You Ain't Lived

'TIL YOU GROW OLD

Lenore Glassman
Yvette Jackson
Illustrated by Kathleen Morris

Second Edition
Lyco Publishing
Houston, Texas

DEDICATED
TO THE FOLKS
WHO RELATE TO THIS BOOK*

*IT'S IN LARGE BOLD PRINT IN CASE
YOU HAVE LOST YOUR GLASSES.

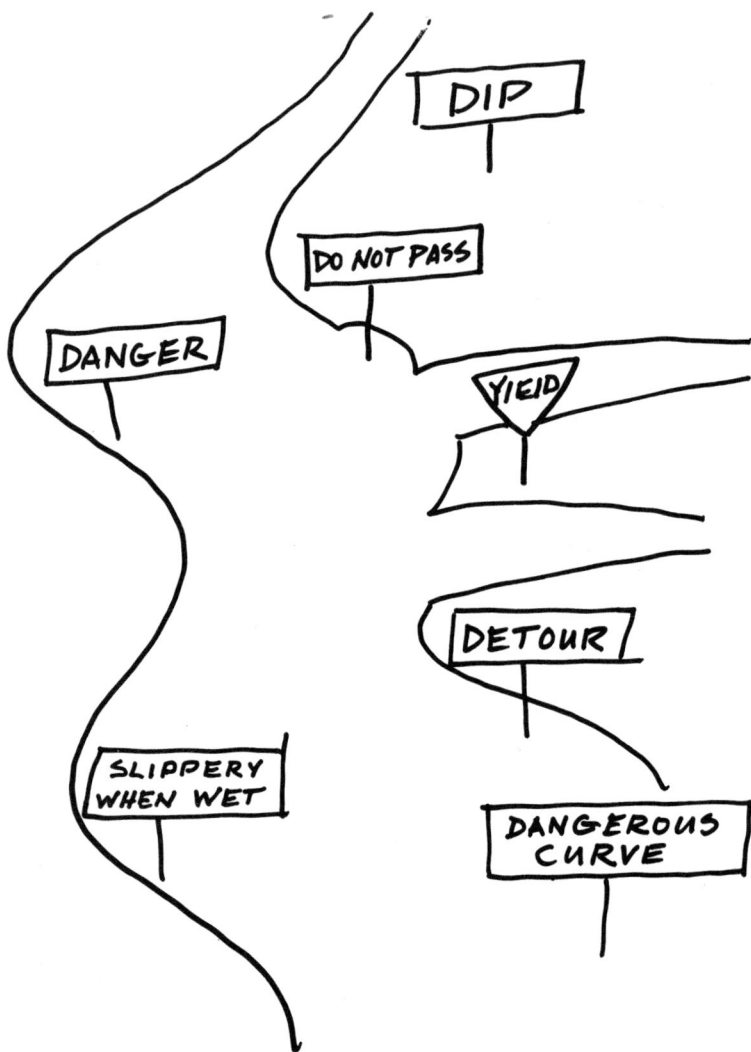

AND IT ALL BEGINS AT 40

HAPPY 40TH BIRTHDAY TO YOU

GOOD NEWS

YOU CAN JOG THREE (3) MILES A DAY

BAD NEWS

YOUR KNEES ARE KILLING YOU

GOOD NEWS

YOU DON'T DRINK BEER

BAD NEWS

YOU HAVE A BEER BELLY

GOOD NEWS

YOU HAVE A WONDERFUL LAUGH

BAD NEWS

IT'S CREASED INTO YOUR FACE

GOOD NEWS
YOUR FRIENDS LOOK LUMPY
IN TENNIS SHORTS

BAD NEWS

SO DO YOU

GOOD NEWS

YOU GET COMPLIMENTS
ON YOUR GOLD CHAINS

BAD NEWS

YOUR HUSBAND IS WEARING THEM

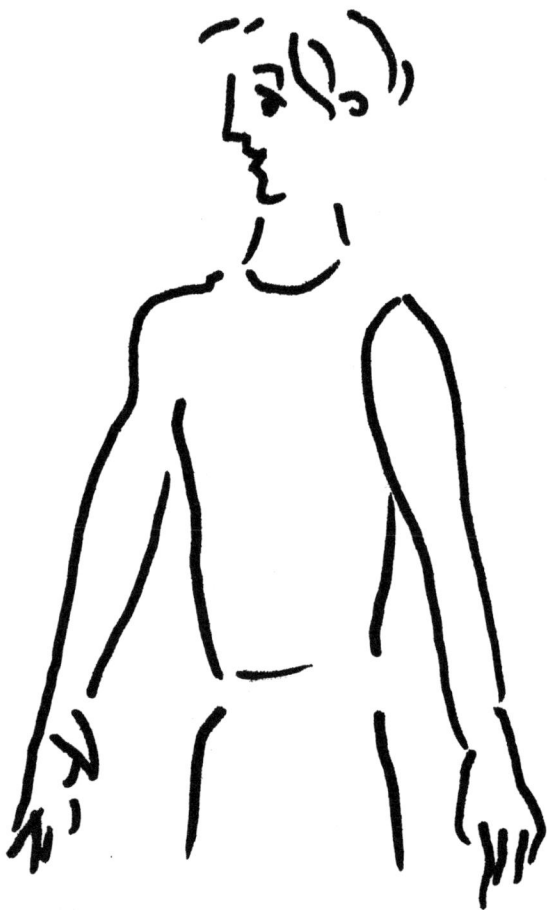

GOOD NEWS

YOUR BABY IS 15

BAD NEWS

EVERYBODY THINKS HE'S YOUR

GRANDCHILD

GOOD NEWS

YOU'RE LOOKING GOOD

BAD NEWS

IT TAKES A DRAWER FULL OF MAKE-UP

GOOD NEWS

YOU DON'T DYE YOUR HAIR

BAD NEWS

YOU STREAK, TINT, HIGHLIGHT OR RINSE

GOOD NEWS

YOU PULL OUT THE GRAY HAIRS

BY THE ROOTS

BAD NEWS

YOU'RE GETTING BALD

GOOD NEWS

DRIED PRUNES HELP

BAD NEWS

YOU'RE BEGINNING TO LOOK LIKE ONE

TEST I

START THIS TEST AT 50.

PLACE RIGHT HAND ON TABLE, PALM DOWN.

WITH LEFT HAND PINCH SKIN ON TOP OF HAND ON TABLE.

THE TIME IT TAKES TO GET BACK TO ORIGINAL SHAPE IS DIRECTLY RELATED TO AGE.

IF YOU NEED A CALENDAR INSTEAD OF A CLOCK, YOU'RE IN TROUBLE.

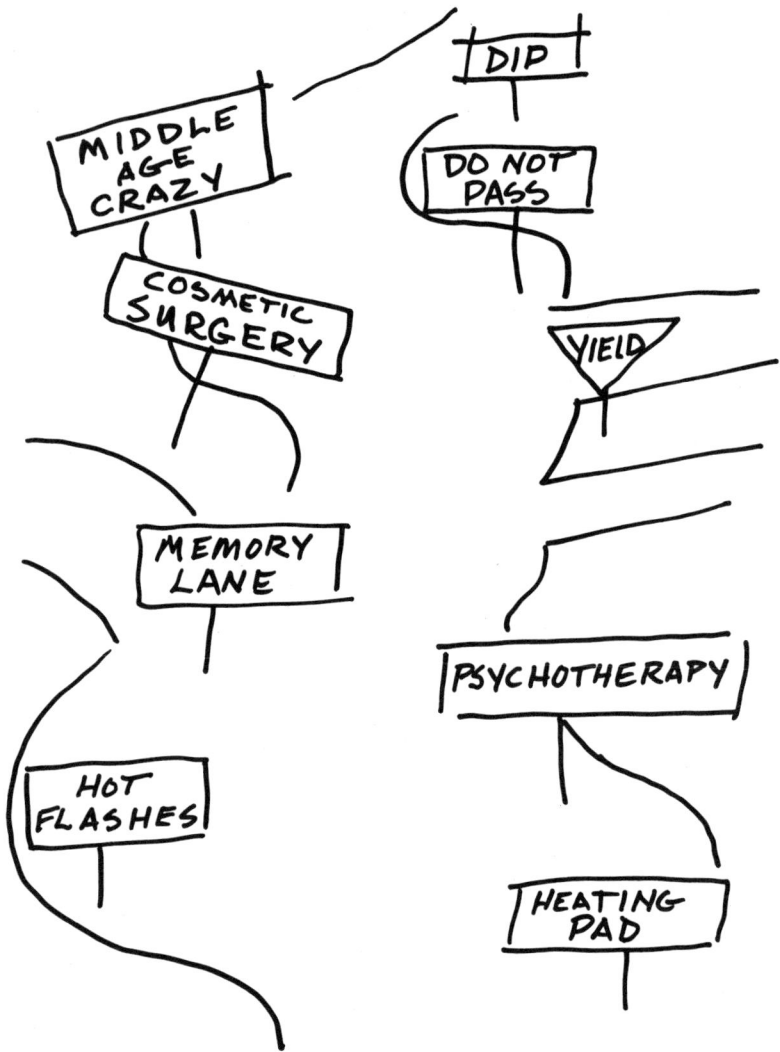

AND INTO YOUR 50'S

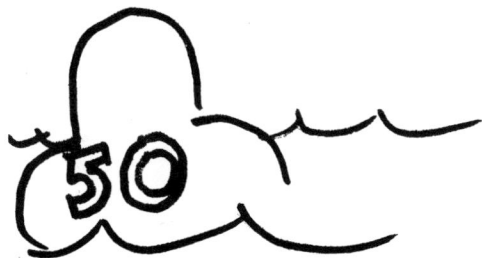

GOOD NEWS

YOU'RE HAVING A BIRTHDAY

HAPPY BIRTHDAY

BAD NEWS

IT'S HALF A CENTURY

GOOD NEWS

YOU HAVE SOME BEAUTIFUL SLIPS

BAD NEWS

THE YOUNG ONES SAY: WHAT'S A SLIP

GOOD NEWS

SLEEVELESS DRESSES ARE IN AGAIN

BAD NEWS

YOUR UPPER ARMS HANG LOOSE

GOOD NEWS

YOU'RE LOOKING GOOD

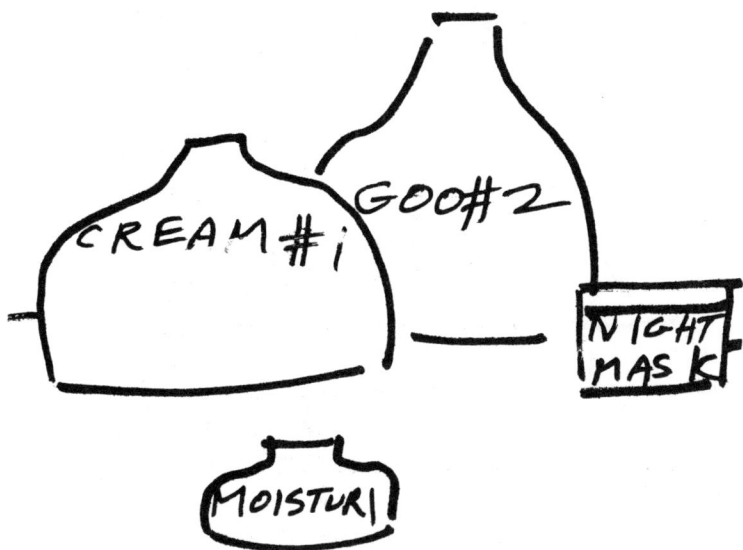

BAD NEWS

IT TAKES A DRAWER FULL OF MOISTURIZERS

GOOD NEWS

YOU HAVE A DRAWER FULL

OF UNDERSHIRTS

BAD NEWS

NOW YOU CALL THEM "T-SHIRTS"

GOOD NEWS

YOU STILL HAVE CUTE LITTLE FRECKLES

BAD NEWS

NOW THEY'RE CALLED BROWN SPOTS

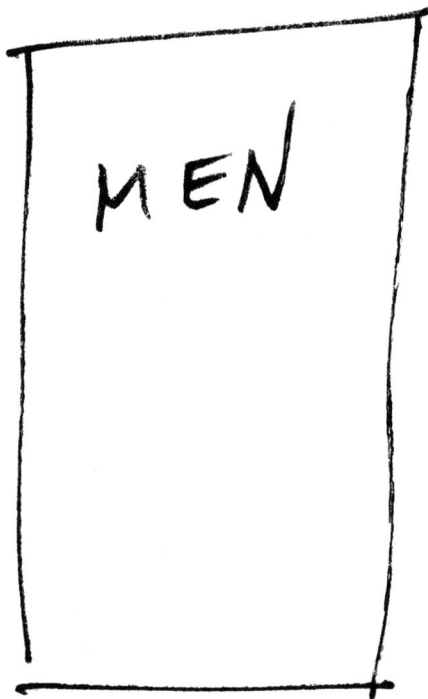

MEN

GOOD NEWS

YOUR BLADDER IS FUNCTIONING WELL

BAD NEWS

A LITTLE TOO WELL

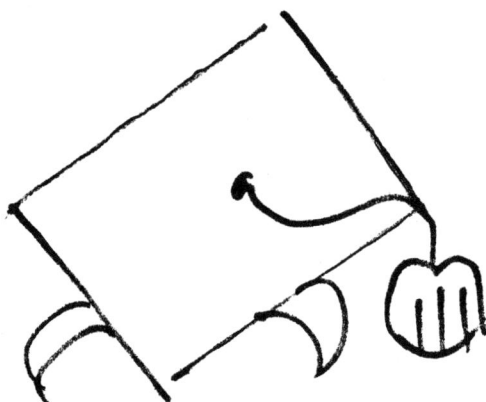

GOOD NEWS

YOUR KIDS ARE ALL GROWN

BAD NEWS

THEY COME FOR LONG VISITS

WITH THEIR KIDS

GOOD NEWS

YOU STILL HAVE A WONDERFUL LAUGH

BAD NEWS

IT'S ETCHED INTO CROW'S FEET

GOOD NEWS

YOU TELL PEOPLE YOU'RE A VETERAN

BAD NEWS

THEY ASK, "WORLD WAR I?"

TEST II

IT IS ADVISABLE TO SIT DOWN FOR THIS TEST.

PLACE HAND MIRROR FLAT ON TABLE -

NOW LEAN OVER, GENTLY, SO FACE IS DIRECTLY OVER MIRROR.

YOU WILL NOTICE YOUR WHOLE FACE FALLS FORWARD.

SUGGESTION: START INVESTIGATING

PLASTIC SURGEONS.

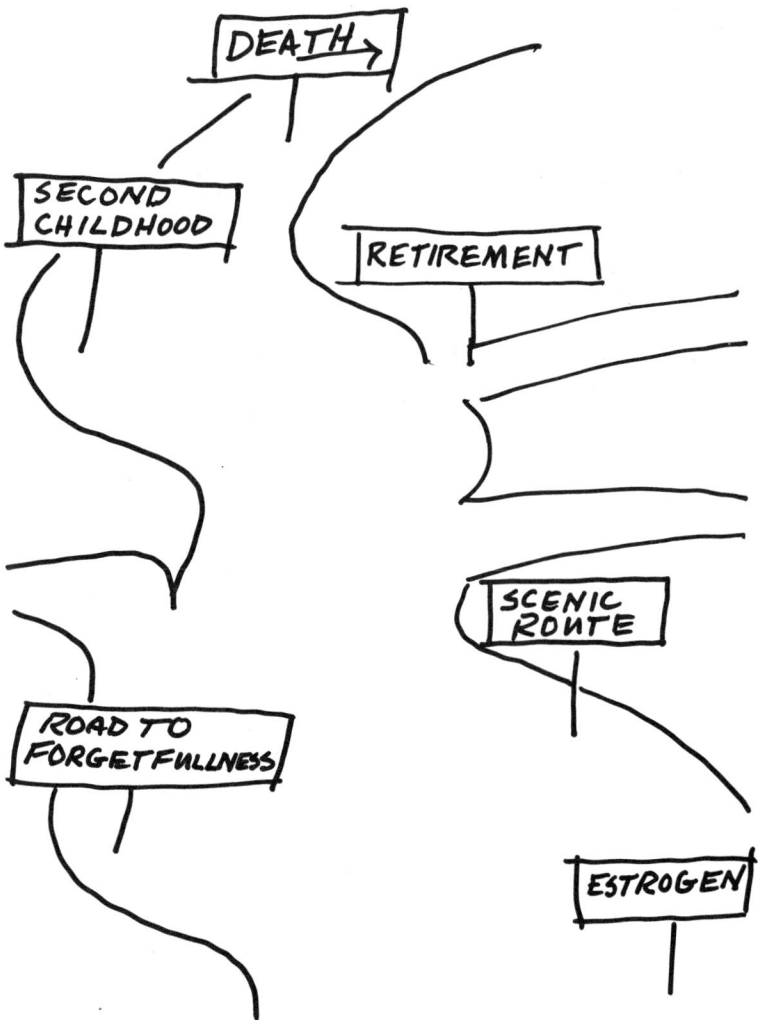

AND HERE COME YOUR 60'S

BEAT IT, KID! I KNOW HOW
TO CROSS THE STREET!

GOOD NEWS

YOU'RE HAVING A BIRTHDAY

50+

50+

50+

$100 \div 2 = 50+$

BAD NEWS

IT'S MORE THAN HALF A CENTURY

10%
OFF FOR
SENIOR
CITIZENS

GOOD NEWS

YOU'RE ELIGIBLE FOR SENIOR CITIZENS'
DISCOUNTS

BAD NEWS

NO ONE ARGUES

GOOD NEWS

YOUR GRANDCHILDREN ARE FANTASTIC

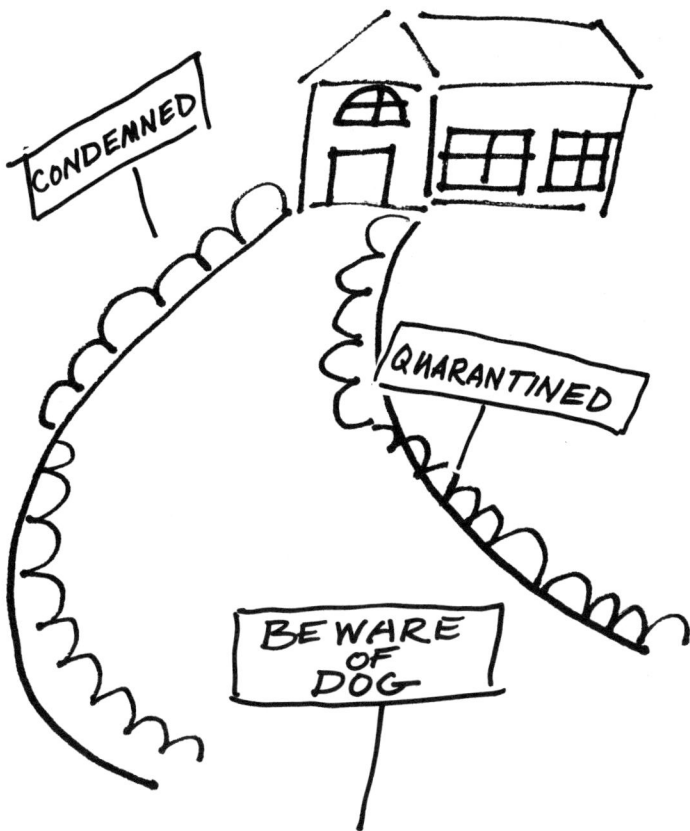

BAD NEWS

THEY CAN WALK OVER TO YOUR HOUSE

GOOD NEWS

YOU FEEL GREAT

BAD NEWS

YOU'RE FROM SHORT LIVED PEOPLE

GOOD NEWS

THERE ARE A LOT OF GOOD BOOKS ON SEX.

BAD NEWS

ALL YOU DO IS READ

YOU ARE
CORDIALLY
INVITED
_ __ _

GOOD NEWS

YOU GO TO A PARTY TO SEE OLD FRIENDS

BAD NEWS

EVERYONE ELSE LOOKS OLD

GOOD NEWS

THERE'S A LOT OF TALKING AND TELLING

BAD NEWS

NOT MUCH DOING AND SCREWING

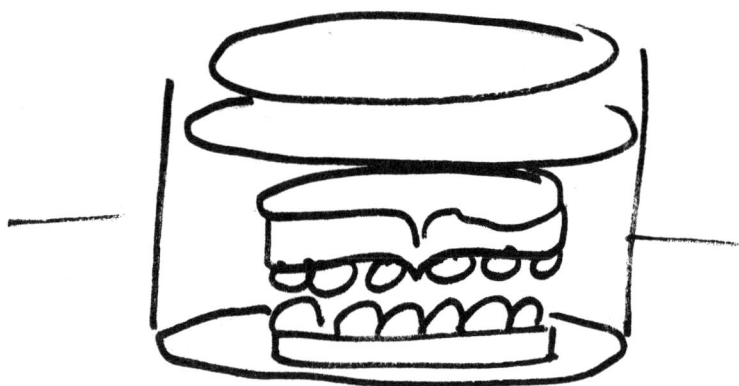

BAD NEWS

YOU LOST YOUR TEETH

GOOD NEWS

YOUR GUMS ARE HEALTHY

GOOD NEWS

YOU'RE A VOLUNTEER IN A HOME

FOR THE AGED

BAD NEWS

**ONE OF THE RESIDENTS ASKS YOU
TO SHARE A ROOM**

GOOD NEWS

YOU'VE ACQUIRED A LOT OF WISDOM

BAD NEWS

NO ONE WANTS YOUR ADVICE

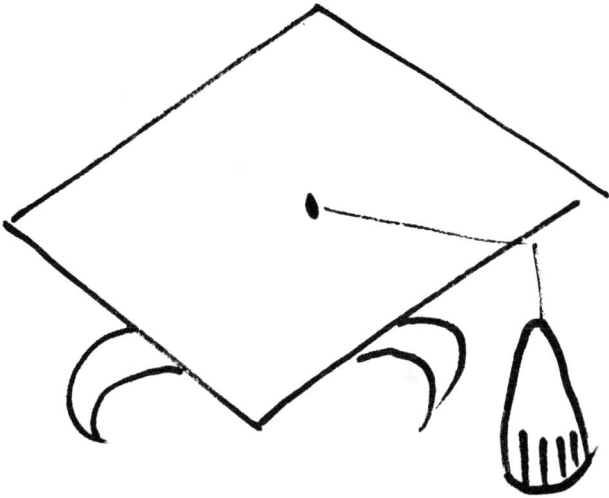

GOOD NEWS

YOUR CHILDREN ARE INDEPENDENT

BAD NEWS

EXCEPT WHEN THEY NEED MONEY

BAD NEWS

YOU'RE IN YOUR 70's

GOOD NEWS

YOU MADE IT TO YOUR 70'S

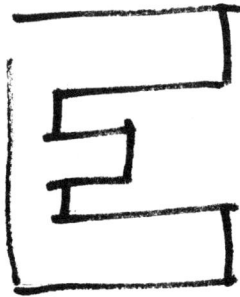

BAD NEWS

YOUR EYES ARE GETTING BAD

GOOD NEWS

YOU CAN'T SEE YOUR WRINKLES

BAD NEWS

IT TAKES LONGER TO GET THERE

GOOD NEWS

YOU GET THERE

BAD NEWS

YOUR PACEMAKER OPENS THE GARAGE

GOOD NEWS

ONLY WHEN A PRETTY GIRL GOES BY

BAD NEWS

YOU GO TO A LOT OF FUNERALS

GOOD NEWS

THEY AIN'T YOURS

BAD NEWS

YOUR SPOUSE LIKES TO SOCIALIZE

GOOD NEWS

YOU CAN SLEEP ANYWHERE

BAD NEWS

PEOPLE THINK YOU HAVE ROCKS

IN YOUR HEAD

GOOD NEWS

THEY SHOULD ONLY KNOW

WHAT YOU'RE THINKING

LAST WILL & TESTAMENT

BAD NEWS

YOUR KIDS REMIND YOU

TO WRITE YOUR WILL

GOOD NEWS

YOU'RE FROM LONG LIVED PEOPLE

BAD NEWS

BODY FUNCTIONS HAVE SLOWED DOWN

GOOD NEWS

DIARRHEA IS A PLEASURE

BAD NEWS

YOUR CHILDREN TELL YOU THEIR TROUBLES

WITH THEIR KIDS

GOOD NEWS

GREAT!

BAD NEWS

THE KIDS ARE ALREADY SPLITTING UP

YOUR GOODIES

SALVATION ARMY

GOOD NEWS

YOU'VE LEFT MOST OF IT

TO THE SALVATION ARMY

BAD NEWS

YOU URINATE FREQUENTLY

GOOD NEWS

YOUR PANTS STAY DRY

GREAT NEWS

**YOU'VE LIVED LONG ENOUGH TO BE
A PROBLEM TO YOUR CHILDREN!**